Quilting for Beginners

The Ultimate Guide to Quilting for Life

Check out what others have been saying about this book.....

"With this book it's been Easier Than ever to begin successfully quilting on a daily basis and it's so much fun!"

- **Heather Todler**

"After reading this book I've finally completed my first quilting project!"

- *Bree Farnson*

"This was the best book on quilting I've read in a long time. It's a pretty simple book but really sums everything up. Thank You!"

- **Michelle Gosslin**

Table of Contents

Introduction

Chapter 1: Understanding Quilting

Chapter 2: Basic Quilting Tips

Chapter 3: Making Your Own Quilt

Conclusion

Bonus Chapter: Crochet Basics

Copyright © 2015

All rights reserved. No part of this book may be reproduced in any form without permission in writing from the author. Reviewers may quote brief passages in reviews.

Disclaimer

No part of this publication may be reproduced or transmitted in any form or by any means, mechanical or electronic, including photocopying or recording, or by any information storage and retrieval system, or transmitted by email without permission in writing from the publisher.

While all attempts and efforts have been made to verify the information held within this publication, neither the author nor the publisher assumes any responsibility for errors, omissions, or opposing interpretations of the content herein.

This book is for entertainment purposes only. The views expressed are those of the author alone, and should not be taken as expert instruction or commands. The reader of this book is responsible for his or her own actions when it comes to reading the book.

Adherence to all applicable laws and regulations, including international, federal, state, and local governing professional licensing, business practices, advertising, and all other aspects of doing business in the US, Canada, or any other jurisdiction is the sole responsibility of the purchaser or reader.

Neither the author nor the publisher assumes any responsibility or liability whatsoever on the behalf of the purchaser or reader of these materials.

Any received slight of any individual or organization is purely unintentional.

Introduction

I want to thank you and congratulate you for downloading the book, **"Quilting for Beginners: The Ultimate Guide to Quilting for Life"**.

This book contains proven steps and strategies for understanding the basic concepts and techniques related to quilting.

Welcome to the world of quilting!

Quilting is a relaxing hobby that can be started by anyone who wants a creative way to spend time. It can help a person create wonderful and artistic pieces that can be of practical use. You can even create family heirlooms or personalized gifts. There are many things you can do once you enter the world of quilting. If you are looking for a new hobby, then quilting might be for you!

This book contains the basic things that you need to know in relation to quilting. Browse through the pages in order to find out how to enjoy this very fun activity.

Thanks again for downloading this book, I hope you enjoy it!

Chapter 1: Understanding Quilting

The art of quilting has been popular since some time in the Middle Ages. History shows that this practice was done in Europe, India, the Far East and in many other parts of the world. Generally speaking, a quilt is two layers of fabric with a filling in between, all held together by stitching. However, there are certain quilting styles which eliminate the fabric in between resulting to just two outer layers sewn together. The kinds of quilt are generally influenced by location and era. Each culture and period has different kinds of quilts.

Homemade quilts are very satisfying to create and it instantly gives a personalized touch to any space. You can add color and design to your home by learning how to make your own quilts. Do you dream of making your own quilts but are clueless as to where and how to start?

Quilting indeed seems like an intimidating hobby. However, it can be easily learned if you have clear instructions and an easy pattern. Expert quilters were once a beginner like you, so you can surely learn the proper technique of quilting with enough time, patience and dedication.

You can approach this new hobby through many different angles. There are many things to learn if you are just trying out quilting for the first time. So you just need to find a starting point that you are comfortable with.

Naturally, you shouldn't start with a complicated project. A basic quilting pattern of a mini quilt is a good starting point. Once you get the basics of construction, composition and stitching, you can move on to more complicated projects. Before you know it you can create patchwork pillows, silhouette quilts and wall hangings. Your home will truly look more beautiful if you have these homemade decors that will give any space a personalized and unique touch.

What is quilting?

In simplest terms, quilting is simply the art of stitching together three layers of cloth to form a decorative design. It can be done by hand or by machine. If you choose to do it by hand, it should be sone in quilting hoop or frame using special needles and a quilting thread. The challenge is to make the stitches straight and uniform. There are also hand stitchers who are proud of their ability to make tiny stitches. On the other hand, machine stitching is done through a regular sewing machine. The challenge usually lies in learning how to smoothly feed the three layers of cloth to the sewing machine.

Each of the methods has advantages and disadvantages in relation to speed, design and quality of work. Machine quilting is faster, more efficient and more ideal for mass production. On the other hand, hand quilting gives the quilt a softer look and it seems to have more dimension than machine quilting.

Patchwork and quilting are two distinct art forms but they can be combined in order to create more beautiful products.

What are the products that I can make with quilting?

The earliest quilting projects were said to be for bedcovers. They were in fact so treasured that they were included in family inventories and were passed on to generations as family heirlooms. In the middle ages, quilts were also used to create warm and fashionable clothes.

The level of skill and artistry of quilters were often praised, and in some countries, there works are considered cultural treasures.

Naturally, if you are just starting out, you don't need to pressure yourself to create something elaborate and very detailed. It is completely understandable if you start out your quilting hobby with something simple like a pillow case or a baby blanket. Eventually, as your skill levels up, you can try focusing on more difficult items.

What are the materials and equipment needed for quilting?

The materials needed for quilting are very basic. Here are some of the things you need if you want to get into hand quilting anytime soon.

1. Fabric- You can get very creative in choosing the perfect fabric for your quilt. You can choose plain or patterned fabrics for the top layer of your quilt to achieve the look that you want. Choose fabrics based on the theme or design that you want to create. You can get very creative with your choices so that your personality and style preferences would come out in your work. Don't forget to purchase something for the backing fabric as well. Usually a light

or medium weight cotton or calico is ideal for the job. For the back part, you have the option to make it quilted or not.

2. Thread- For a better quality of work, it is best to choose threads that are specifically made for quilting. They are easily available and you can purchase them in hobby or specialty stores. The key is to try and create an overall look for your quilt. You must choose a thread that will match the fabrics that you chose. If you will use different colors of fabric, you can choose different threads for each part. You can also opt for just one thread color which matches the predominant fabric in your quilt. In modern quilts, the trend is to choose a thread in color in contrast to the color of the fabric.

3. Needles and pins- Just like a specialized thread, you also need a specialized needle for quilting. This will make the sewing mud easier and more efficient. Also, you need a lot pins which are essential for good patchwork. Use pins that are light and rust-free. It is advisable to go for colored pins so that they will be a easier to find, especially if you are working on a large fabric. Traditional needles for patchwork are shorter than ordinary needles but they are also sharper. Make sure that you choose the right size so that it would be easier for you to secure the fabric that you are sewing.

4. Scissors and cutting equipment- There are several things which could make quilting easier for you. You can invest in a rotary cutter, a quilter's rule and a self-cutting mat in order to cut fabrics and templates according to the design you want. Alternatively, you can use ordinary sewing or dressmaking scissors to cut individual pieces for your design.

5. Other quilting equipment- Generally speaking, the four items mentioned above are the only things you need to get started on your quilting journey. However, you might want to invest in other things that can help make your quilting journey more fun and exciting. Patchwork templates, hoops, fabric markers and frames are needed for more complex patterns and patchwork. As you progress, you may also want to invest in a sewing machine that will allow you to finish more quilts in a shorter amount of time.

Quilting terms

Just like any activity, you need to understand several quilting terms which can help you understand what you are doing. It will be easier for you to follow instructions if you know how exactly each step goes.

Here are some quilting terms that you will surely encounter in your quilting experience.

Quilting- This is the process of securing together the three layers of the quilt. This includes the top layer (where the design and pattern can be seen), the filler (sometimes called the wadding) and the backing fabric. It may be done with a simple backing stitch or with the help of a sewing machine.

When you are just starting out, you can make the stitching a simple running stitch. However, as your skills improve, you can move to more complicated ones. Eventually, you can add intertwining cables, lines and patterns. There are many available patterns that can guide you in achieving the design you want.

Patchwork- Patchwork is the element of quilting which makes it beautiful and unique. It is the process of cutting shapes from different fabric and putting them together to form a design you want. Through the patchwork, you can truly allow your creativity to come out. You can choose any fabric you want and any color which you think will suit the design. You can use a traditional or a modern approach. The possibilities are truly endless. The uniqueness of your quilt will truly come out in your fabric and color choices.

A rotary cutter is useful in cutting uniform-sized pieces all at once. However, a sewing scissors is just fine. The pieces of fabric may be sewn together by hand or by machine. You will be able to achieve a fantastic design just by simply putting together the right color and kind of fabric.

Tacking- While you are sewing together the three layers of your quilt, it is essential to try and hold them together. You can do this through a process called tacking or basting. It's like temporarily holding together the quilt as you properly sew the layers together. This step makes the process of quilting much easier. Tacking usually means using long hand-stitches to hod the layers together. However, you also have the option to use curved basting pins or a basting gun for quick work.

***Wadding*-** Wadding is the thick piece of cloth sandwiched between the two outer layers of cloth. It is usually made of cotton, polyester or a blend of both. When you are just starting out, it is bet to use thin wadding so that you can control and maneuver the quilt more easily.

***Wholecloth quilt*-** Just as the name suggests, a wholecloth quilt is a kind of quilt made from whole cloth. It's just like having two pieces of fabric with a wadding between them. However, the thread and the stitching still gives the quilt a pattern so it can still look personalized and unique.

***Appliqué*-** This is another element of the quilt which can bring out your creative side. Appliqués can allow you to add anything you want to add to your design. You can put in a flower, an animal, a shape...anything that interests you! You can make a special, personalized appliqué if you want a unique grift for someone special. You can sew in the appliqués by hand or with the help of a sewing machine.

Chapter 2: Basic Quilting Tips

While there is a lot of room for creativity when quilting, you have to keep in mind that you need to follow certain rules as well. It involves learning skills and techniques that will enable you to come up with a nice quilt.

Quilting traditions have changed a lot in the past years. The technique used by traditional quilters in the middle ages are probably different from the techniques used of quilters now. Thanks to modern technology, you have the option to make your quilting experience a lot easier.

Here are some tips that you need to know and understand as you begin your quilting journey.

1. Learn to read quilting patterns

When you are still starting out, it is best to stick to simple and basic patterns until you get the hang of what you are supposed to do. Quilting patterns will make you familiar with how to do a particular technique. It will also allow you to be familiar with the terms and lingo used in the quilting world. You can start with simple block pattern and move on to more difficult projects once you feel that your skills have improved.

2. Understand the concepts behind quilting fabrics

Fabric is the skeleton of your quilts, so you must try to understand how quilts work in order to choose what is the best for your quilt. You can just use any fabric for your quilting projects. Generally speaking, the most convenient fabric to use is cotton because it is easy to use and sew.

You have to understand some concepts related to fabric like fabric grain and bleed test. Fabric grain simply pertains to way the thread is arranged. With the right fabric grain, it will be much easier for you to create quilt blocks that are accurate and easy to assemble.

You also have to understand how to do a bleed test. Some fabrics, especially the ones with vibrant colors, can bleed or lose their colors when washed, This can lead to a disaster! Aside from staining other clothing in your wash load, you can ruin a quilt that took ages to make. So it is best to conduct bleed tests until you know which fabrics work for you. Most fabrics made by modern manufacturers no longer bleed but it is still best to check to avoid any mishaps.

Another thing that you have to consider is the importance of pre-washing. Pre-washing your fabric will help you avoid any surprises when you wash your quilt for the first time. When you pre-wash your fabric, you will easily be able to tell if it bleeds. In addition to this, you will also be able to tell if it shrinks. This will allow you determine if a certain fabric choice is suitable for our quilt project. It is better to know that your fabric is not suitable for a quilt before you start working.

3. Getting comfortable with color

It is a good idea to familiarize yourself with the color wheel to know which colors match. When you walk into a fabric store for the first time, there is a good chance that you will be bombarded with different hues, shades and patterns. It might be difficult to decide what you want if you are clueless on how to choose well.

Color and pattern value are important because you need to see the relationship of a particular choice to the other parts of the quilt. Keep in mind that you trying to create a full design, so you must try to see the whole picture. Even if you really want a particular fabric, if it doesn't match the rest of your quilt, then you better just reserve it for another project. The design of your quilt is dependent on how well you are able to put the colors and patterns of your fabric together. This is where your creativity will truly come out.

4. Understanding quilt block construction

Identifying and analyzing the patchwork block construction of your quilt will allow you to create your quilts with symmetrical design. In a nutshell, you can recognize a quilt block by the arrangement of their patches. It is not unlike a graphing paper, and you can categorize the blocks as four-patch, nine-patch and five patch. Once you get the hang of understanding this design concept, it will be much easier for you to play around and come up with a design that is uniquely yours.

Four-patch grids are the most common and they are probably the easiest to handle for beginners. A four-patch grid is actually arranged in a two by two format. The blocks can still be subdivided further but it is important to still be able to understand and recognize the four-patch structure for symmetry of the design. As your quilting skills improve, you can move on to the nine-patch grid and the five-patch grid.

As you study quilt block construction, you have to learn accurate pressing as well in order to help you create the design you want. You'll find that your quilt will look more neat if the blocks are all in the same size and if they fit together really well.

5. *Study quilt layouts*

You'll find that depending on what you want to do, you will need to study various quilt layouts in order to select the correct pattern for what you want to create. Quilting a pillowcase is different from quilting a mattress, so you should study what suits the patterns best.

For example, when you choose to quilt a mattress, there are things to consider other than the design of the quilt. What is the size of the mattress? Does it have a footboard? What are the dimensions? Consider all these things because precise measurement is essential in creating the perfect quilt.

6. *Think about borders and sashing*

Aside from the pattern and design of the quilt, you must also consider the border and sashing which will affect the overall look of your quilt. The most common border type are straight sewn borders because they are easy to sew. If you want something unique, you might want to go for pierced borders or a border print that will add a creative touch to your final product.

7. *Keep practicing*

Just like any skill, you will become a better quilter with time, effort and practice. At the beginning, it might seem all too confusing because there are many decisions that you need to make. However, you will get a better understanding of the process the more you do it.

You should always start with the basic and most simple options. Then, as your skill increases, you can start exploring the other options. Do not be overwhelmed by the various options available for you. Instead of being intimidated, you can think of these as ways to be creative as your skill level improves.

Also, try to level your expectations when you are just starting out. You can't expect to finish a full-blown complicated project on your first try. You might end up turning your back on quilting if you don't like your first creation. Just start simple and work your way up.

8. Take a beginner class or join a community

While it is nice to learn a skill all by yourself, you might find it difficult or frustrating. One thing that you can do to help have a smoother start when it comes to quilting is to join a class or join a community of quilters. There are a lot of benefits in learning a new skill with a group of people.

You will be guaranteed that what you are doing is correct because there are experts who can guide you as you make your quilts. As such, you might find yourself more enthusiastic about the projects because you have people who can guide you as you progress. You can also share materials with the people you are learning with, so you don't have to worry about investing in so much quilting paraphernalia. Lastly, you can make friends with the women you are learning with. This makes the experience much more fun and interesting for you because you can share it with others.

Chapter 3: Making Your Own Quilt

Quilting is a fun and exciting way to bring out your creative side. It can bring personal fulfillment to people of all ages and skill level. The best part of it is that when you know how to quilt, you can create practical items that you can give as gifts or you can use in your home. You can even create something that could be considered a family heirloom that can be passed on from generation to generation.

Making a quilt is a dry hands-on experience. It can be a time-consuming process but it is something that will give you personal fulfillment. The best thing to do is to give yourself time to actually learn the process. Even experts don't rush making their quilts. Try to enjoy the process and understand what you need to do in every step.

Do you think you are ready for making your own quilt?

The only way you can truly learn how to quilt is by making one. No matter how many tips you read, you won't fully understand them if you don't actually apply what you are reading. It's time to get your hands dirty. Gather your supplies and start quilting!

Here are the things that you should do. These are the very basic steps of quilting which could help you get started.

1. *Decide on a pattern*

Once you are an expert quilter, you will no longer need a pattern in order to come up with beautiful designs, but sine you are just starting out, you might want to consider using an easy pattern that can guide you with your creation. For those who are just starting out, it is easiest to choose a blanket made of quilted rows.

2. *Wash and press the fabric.*

As mentioned earlier you need to make sure that your fabric is perfect for your quilt even before you start sewing. You can do this by washing and pressing the fabric first.

Pre-washing will allow you to determine if your fabric will bleed or shrink. Generally speaking, higher-quality fabric will not, but it is best to check nonetheless. Pressing the fabric will allow for easier cutting.

You don't need to press the wadding. Only the two outer layers need to be ironed.

3. Measure accordingly

Measure the size of the individual pieces that you need to complete the pattern. Don't forget to add allowance for the seam. Usually, a 1/4 inch allowance is needed. This means that you need to add 1/4 inch on each side of the square. For example, if the requirement is 5 inches per side, you need to create pieces that measures 5 1/2 inch by 5 1/2 inch. This will be easier if you have a ruler and a washable fabric pen to mark the measurements before cutting.

4. Start cutting

Make sure you measure everything twice before cutting to avoid mistakes. If you have a rotary blade and a cutting mat, lay the fabric on top of one another on the mat and cut accordingly with the guidance of a ruler. If you are using scissors, cut the fabric one by one, and make sure that you follow the markings to made to keep the edges straight.

5. Sew the squares together

You can practice arranging the fabric and designs before you sew the cut pieces of square together. Lay your quilt just so you can see the pattern that you are trying to create.

Pin the individual squares together so that it will be easier for you to sew. Whether you are using your hand or the machine, the point is to just sew the squares together until you come up with long, thin strips. Work your way across the quilt until you come up with one row. You can then proceed to completing the next row afterwards. Make sure that you are sewing the rows together at exactly 1/4 inch. You should have several rows of squares after this step.

6. Sew the rows together

Now that you have several rows of squares, you have to sew the rows together. The process is still the same, but instead of just square pieces, you are now going to sew together the rows of square pieces that you made earlier. Work your way downwards. Make sure that you are still keeping the 1/4 inch allowance for the seam. Just keep on adding rows until you complete the quilt. If you find that the square pieces don't exactly line up, it's okay. It will give your quilt a personalized touch.

You now have the front layer of your quilt.

7. Baste the quilt

Pin your quilt in place before sewing. You can use pins or a basting gun for this step. Keep the quilt you just created in front, the wadding in the middle and backing pattern at the back. Make sure that the pins are secure, and try to remove any wrinkles on the quilt to make the sewing process much easier.

8. Sew the layers together

Before sewing the quilt together make sure that everything is in the right place. The more seams you sew through the quilt, the better your quilt will be because it will be hard to move. More seams will also prevent bunching up inside the the quilt. You also have the option to sew the seams diagonally or to sew freehand to add a personalized touch to what you are doing. However, if you are not yet completely confident about your sewing skills,it is best to apply the pattern first.

9. Sew the binding

The binding is like the border of the fabric. Aside from adding to the aesthetic quality of your quilt, it will protect the seams and add a more finished look. It should be around 2 1/2 inches wide and it should go around the perimeter of your quilt. For something square, cut four strips of equal length.

Before you sew the binding. pin them in place first so that it wont move around as you sew. Use as much pins as you need to secure the binding in place. Start with sewing the front of the binding. If you are using a printed binding, make sure that you are showing the printed side.

The tricky party of sewing the binding is sewing the back part because there is a chance that the stitches will show at the front. In order to prevent this, you can use an invisible thread or you can opt to hand stitch so that the stitches will look neat. Try to avoid going through all three layers of the quilt.

As you finish the basting, make sure that you have even seams. You should also check if the corners are squared off.

10. Wash your quilt

Your quilt is now finished!

Before using it, wash it first so that it will have a soft and vintage feel. It will also allow you to see if you will encounter any problems before using the quilt. Now you can admire your work and be proud of yourself for finishing your very own handmade quilt.

Conclusion

Thank you again for downloading this book!

I hope this book was able to help you to introduce you to the wonderful world of quilting.

The next step is to go ahead and buy your supplies. Make sure to choose patterns and colors that will truly bring out your personality and style. Also, try to keep things simpleton your first try. If you are able to complete a beautiful quilt the first time you try it, then you can move on to a more complicated pattern. However, if you are not satisfied with your first creation, try and try again until you come up with something that you are satisfied with.

Finally, if you enjoyed this book, please take the time to share your thoughts and post a review on Amazon. It'd be greatly appreciated!

Thank you and good luck!

Bonus Chapter: Crochet Basics

Some might think that crocheting is a seemingly forgotten skill. This intricate and highly personalized art form is now being replaced by computerized sewing machines and digital printing. Fortunately, there are a few who believe that crocheting is making a comeback. Some might even say that it never really went away.

The current trends which call for a simpler lifestyle allow us to appreciate simpler things more fully. Even the younger generations have found a new way to appreciate crocheting. It is good to know this seemingly forgotten art form won't completely go away anytime soon.

Although no one really knows when and where this art form originated, the first known historical records related to crochet date back to the 1800's. It was even believed that there was a time when hands and fingers were used in lieu of hooks which weren't available back then. For a while it was considered the pastime of the upper class because it was believed that the poor ones have no need for luxurious crocheted items. Even Queen Victoria learned how to crochet! It is truly a hobby that binds women from various generations and cultures.

Nowadays, new styles and techniques are still being developed by modern-day crocheters. It is an ever-changing art form that has not yet lost its appeal.

In a sense, the appeal of crocheting increased because high quality yarns and hooks became more easily available at a friendlier price. In this time of economic difficulties, crocheting is a good creative outlet which doesn't require a lot of investment. All you really need are a hook and some yarn. It is a practical way to add interesting and creative elements to your home or your wardrobe. You can even make handmade gifts if you know how to crochet. Crocheted products are beautiful, practical and personalized. Surely, they are unlike any other items which you'll find in malls and stores.

Is it time for you to learn the art which has kept grandma busy over the years? Do you think that crocheting is for you?

Anytime is a good time to learn how to crochet. Even if you are just a beginner or even if you don't consider yourself crafty at all, it is possible to come up with interesting designs that will highlight your creative side. There are many unique and useful items which you can make even if you only know the basic stitches. It is very easy to learn. You will be amazed by what you can come up with in just a matter of days!

Those who know how to crochet will tell you how it provides a wonderful opportunity for relaxation. As you learn the technique, you will appreciate the calming effect it would give you. At the end of a busy day, crocheting is a good way to forget about your stress. It's amazing how calming it is to achieve work using your hands.

One of the greatest advantages of crocheting is that it is such an inexpensive hobby. With less than a hundred dollars, you can buy enough crocheting tools to last you for years! Compared to other hobbies, crocheting is definitely a much cheaper option. Even if you are just starting out, you don't need to spend much on materials. There is even a good chance that your mother and grandmother would lovingly give you some of theirs.

Even if crocheting is a seemingly simple hobby, it will still allow you to be creative with your hands. If you are one of those artistic types who always need to do something creative, then you might want to give crocheting a chance. Satisfy your creative urges by whipping out your crochet hook and yarn. Come up with a sweater, a pot holder or a bed cover! Surely, the items you end up with will be one of a kind.

Can you imagine painting on a canvas while waiting for your turn in the bank? Do you think that you can bring all your art supplies with you? Very few artistic hobbies are as portable as crocheting. If you know that you are going to have a long ride or you'll need to endure a long wait, you might as well stuff your hook and yarn and you can crochet anytime, anywhere. It's really a no fuss hobby!

Learning how to crochet is a good way to exercise and move your fingers. It is particularly popular with the "mature" ones since it gives them a chance to keep their hands healthy even as they age. Why not start exercising your hands now? Keeping a hobby like this will surely keep your hands in a good working condition even as you grown old.

Crocheting 101

What is the difference between crocheting and knitting?

It is easy to confuse crocheting and knitting but these two differ in technique and in application. Many claim that for beginners, crocheting is easier to learn.

Knitting requires two needles while crocheting needs only one hook. In crochet, there are many different stitches -including four basic stitches- which you can use in coming up with your final product. On the other hand, when you knit, there are only two stitches to choose from. Generally speaking, crocheted items are heavier and bulkier than knitted items so the art you should learn should depend on the items that you want to create.

It is advisable to learn one skill at a time. Just understanding the basics will be enough for you to choose which handiwork you find more enjoyable. If you like both, then try to figure out which items are more appropriate for crocheting and which ones are more appropriate for knitting. In no time, you'll find yourself making gifts for your friends and loved ones!

What items do I need to start crocheting?

Even if you are new to the word of crocheting, the good news is that you won't find yourself overwhelmed by all the supply options that you'll find in the market today. Crochet supplies are so simple and straightforward. This means that you can walk in a store, choose your items and complete your transaction in five minutes!

In essence, all you need are some fiber (usually yarn or crochet thread), a hook and a pair of scissors. That's it!

Since you are only investing in a few materials, it is best to choose high-quality ones in order to enjoy your crocheting experience more. Here are some tips which can help you in your shopping.

It's a good idea to invest in hooks of various sizes in order to figure out which ones you find most comfortable. For starters, you can buy a crochet hook set to ensure that the basic hook sizes are covered. You can choose from materials including bamboo, acrylic, aluminum and steel.

If you are buying only one hook, keep in mind that the size of the hook depends on the size of the yarn. Generally speaking, the thicker the yarn, the bigger the hook will be. Yarns are generally labeled to let buyers know what hooks will match. Just make sure that you pick the right hook size to avoid difficulties.

You might think that color is the most important consideration when buying a yarn. While this is indeed important, there are other things that you must consider when choosing your yarn. Yarn texture, yarn weight and yarn material are just some of the things that you should look into when choosing what yarn to buy. Some materials are simply easier to work with. Instead of buying loads of yarn in the same material, try experimenting at first. Buy a few yards of various yarn materials in order to discover which ones you are most comfortable working with.

Here are some of the most popular yarn materials available in the market today.

Soft-acrylic yarn- This is probably the cheapest option there is, so it is good for beginners who want to play around and practice. It's ideal for those who just want to test the waters. However, this is not a very good material for making presents. For your handmade gifts, you might want to invest in better supplies.

Cotton yarn- Cotton yarn is good for items which you think you will use and wash often like dishcloths. There is also high-quality cotton yarn which is ideal for clothing items. This is a good kind for handmade gifts because cotton allergies are not very common. Keep in mind that for baby items, an even more specialized kind of cotton yarn is available.

Novelty yarn- This is the most expensive kind of yarn, and it probably create the softest items too. Unfortunately, items made from novelty yarn cannot be washed very often as items made from cotton yarn. Novelty yarns are often used to make soft items such as sweaters and scarves.

What should I make first?

It can be overwhelming to start a handiwork when there are so many options to choose from. What will you start with? A hat? A baby blanket? A sweater? Don't overwhelm yourself! Choose a beginner's pattern first and just choose more difficult patterns as your skill progresses. For starters, it is good to try a baby blanket or a scarf.

There are beginner sets which already come with a pattern, some yarn and a hook. These are perfect for beginners because everything you need is already in the set. The difficulty level is surely appropriate for beginners as well.

Where do I start?

After you've purchased all the things you need for your crochet project, the next thing to do is to just tie the leap and start working your hands. If you have some extra yarn, start with playing around and learning the basic stitches. The most important thing is to learn how to be hold the yarn. There is really no single way to do this, and you'll eventually find a position that will make you feel comfortable as you stitch. Here are some of the most common hand-holding techniques used in crocheting.

Over-the-hook position- When you hold the hook this way, it's just like you are holding a pencil. The hook would rest on the palm and you'd rest your thumb and index finger on the on the indentation in the handle (the thumb rest)

Under-the-hook position- On the other hand, when you use the under-the-hook position, it's going to feel like you are holding a spatula and your hand should be resting under the hook. Just like in the over-the-hook position, your thumb and index finger should be resting on the thumb rest.

The experience of crocheting would really be more fun if you have a friend or relative who share the same passion. Perhaps this is a chance for you to re-connect with your mother or grandmother. Maybe it's a new thing that you can share with your friends. Try to find someone who would probably share the same interest in crocheting in order to make the experience more fun!

Made in the USA
Coppell, TX
28 December 2023